"MY CHILDREN

DON'T EAT DOG FOOD"

Natural Recipes for Pets

By: Sandra Kay Hughes

Kaye-Hughes Publishing

© Copyright April 1999
ISBN 0-9674110-0-9

This is quite an unusual natural foods recipe book for the special animal children in all our lives.

It goes beyond cooking for them. I hope to open your eyes and hearts to alternative natural remedies. Remedies to many health related problems that your animal child may be experiencing, or could experience in the future.

Potential hazards to their health and safety are discussed in this book. Including flea treatments.

This is my contribution to the wonderful world of pets, little children that bring far more to us than just companionship. If you let them, they can even heal your heart.

Let me help you give a little back to them, and at the same time extend their lives.

This book is dedicated to the canine love
of my life

My darling Cassie girl.

She is 12 years old as of this writing.
Curled up at my feet as I write, of course.
She has given me her unconditional love
and devotion all these years. Even
through all the adversity in her little,
short life.

This is her story, and mine, of how true
love and devotion and caring can find a
way, when it seems there is no way.
All who know her have come to love her.

What a great gift she is.

I must thank my family of friends, who supported my desire to write, and encouraged me to write this little book of discoveries and solutions to good animal health, that I have personally researched and experimented with through the years.

All who know me, know the love and devotion that I have for Cassie, and it was just a normal course of events for me to begin a search for alternatives, when I was told she would die soon due to inoperable tumors.

With God's help, I will accomplish one of my goals in life, and that is helping all the animal lovers out there keep these precious children of ours healthier and happier and free of disabilities.

Do not lose hope, ever, that there is a solution to whatever ails your best friend. Cassie is living proof that prayer, faith and natural resources can make a difference. I hope to shorten your search for these sources and give you hope too.

A special thanks to Laura Karth, Maryann Baxter, Senior Editors. Sarah Runcie, Linda Swink, my wonderful editorial and computer support. Many thanks to Suzette Williams, Illustrator, and friend. Without whom these adorable pictures would not have appeared.

Welcome to my home, and to my life with animals. Come in and sit for awhile, I need to share a few things with you. I want to make all of you out there aware of alternative medicines, as well as nutritious foods for pets. Without good health our animal children will not, and are not living as long as God intended for them to live, and if I personally can help extend the lives of our precious babies, through you, then I have accomplished what I have set out to do.

My loyal loving friend deserves the best. She deserves to eat healthy, nutritious food just as we do. We would not feed our human children a "by products" dinner, a fancy name to describe what is only fit for the garbage disposal.

So you know, these "by products" are chicken feet, claws, guts, brains, skin, beaks, etc. It turns my stomach to think that I have been feeding my pets food not fit for man or beast. Cat, and dog food is 74% to 78% WATER in most cans. Read the labels.

When rice is listed, as part of the menu on the label, it is only fractionalized grains, bits and pieces of rice in the food. That is why cats need digestive enzymes added to their diet if you are feeding them commercial food. Water and rice chips are a poor diet.

Many cats become anemic due to the lack of nutrition in commercial food.

My animal babies deserve to eat the way God intended for them to eat. Grains, vegetables, fruit, fish, meat, chicken, just as they ate for centuries before man decided to make a profit on animals, and made opening a can away of life for our pet.

I really doubt that Noah stocked the Ark with canned food for 40 days and 40 nights. The earth provided all they needed for their animals.

I assume Jesus did not carry a bag of kibbles with him while he was shepherding the flocks. The sheep dogs ate off the land, ate raw meals, grains, fruits and vegetables.

People have had pets as companions for centuries, but most people of today just do what is easiest and fastest for their pets, because of our busy lives and work schedules. But it is causing many, many diseases and conditions in the bodies of the most loyal friend you will ever have.

We have also blamed most of the diseases, tumors, hip displasia, skin problems, personality disorders, etc. on inbreeding alone. Little does the population know that what they have been feeding them is terribly lacking in nutrition and vitamins and minerals that they need to grow healthy, well balanced and strong from the very start. This poor nutrition can show up in reproduction.

But if we look at the population as a whole, we humans have been taught to eat incorrectly for the last 30 years, by driving to it, microwaving it, or fast fooding it. And we are now fatter than we have ever been.

Our animals only fit into our busy life if we can feed them in five minutes.

Thank God for the naturopaths and holistic medicine in the past five years. We are seeing more and more natural pet veterinarians opening clinics. And some have had their eyes opened to the dangers of years of unnecessary vaccines and poor quality food products for animals while in the field of general vet medicine.

Naturopaths have decided to quit giving pets too many vaccines, vaccines that are not even necessary as they get older. We don't get measles shots every two years, a mumps vaccine every three years, or a polio shot every three years. Our pets have become unwilling victims of the desire to make more money.

I have made it a mission for the rest of my life to tell people how they can promote healthier, longer lives for their beloved companions.

After all, they will go to the ends of the earth for you, and give you complete, total, unconditional love. Where can you find that kind of devotion on this planet? Let's return that unconditional love.

Most humans love you, conditionally, and if you don't make them happy after living with you a couple of years, you become expendable. Not in the animal kingdom. That thought never even enters our pet's minds. There is no 50% divorce rate for animals. Actually, if they could become glued to you at the hip, that would suit our animal children just fine.

Your animal child will live under a bridge with you, eat out of garbage cans, or go hungry with you, sleep wherever you sleep, walk for miles with you to find shelter, then curl up next to you to protect you from harm.

He will spend hours sitting quietly in a car just watching the door, eagerly awaiting the sight of his favorite friend in the whole world.

You **are** his whole world.

He won't care what you look like in the morning, how bad your breath smells, how well you dress for the day, what kind of car you drive, or how rich or famous you are. He is so at peace just being with you and getting an occasional hug or stroking. You have made his day by just existing.

Does this sound like a friend that deserves the best? You bet!

I compiled my favorite recipes for our animal children by taking the best ingredients from many different sources and practicing on my pets to see what improves their health. Most of these recipes have been developed for babies that are battling health problems, but it only stands to reason, that each dish could extend even the life of children that appear to be healthy at this stage.

My little Cassie has a tumor in each adrenal gland, which I will always believe was caused by medication with cortisone in it.

She had a chronic yeast infestation in her ears, due to mold. The dermatologist prescribed medication with cortisone in it, which could have caused the adrenal gland tumors. Adrenal glands produce cortisone for the body.

I was innocent up until a few years ago about medications that are given to our pets. I was also unaware that natural herbs and vitamins would work just as well in animals as they do in humans. After all, most everything is tested on animals first, is it not?

In 1998 1 was told that she would be dead in a few months, but it has been one year now that I found out about the tumors, and she is still with me. She turned 12 in April, 1999.

After switching to holistic natural foods, veggies, fruit, lots of vitamin C and E, garlic, parsley and more, she is a different person (animal, excuse me). She seems to feel wonderful and happy. And the yeast in her ears has completely disappeared, mostly due to the air purification system that I mention later on in the book. I have ozone and needlepoint ionization running 24 hours a day.

I know the end is coming some day, but if I can prolong her life a few more years, keep her happy, healthier, pain free, and if she still has a joy for living, then I owe it to her not to give up. She has never given up on me. She would follow me to the end of time.....if she could.

I want to share the information that I have collected in the

last five years, as I have made it my business to find the best alternative medicines and foods that are out there for my animal children.

Not many veterinarians have come around to this way of thinking, as it does not make them very much money to keep an animal healthy. Right? Naturopaths will tell you that herbs are very inexpensive. The only way they make money is when an animal is sick. Even then, the office visit is usually the most expensive item on the bill.

Even before Cassie was diagnosed I felt I had to give her the best food I could find if she was going to stay healthy for many years. The more I researched commercial food, I knew that I was right. It would keep her unhealthy.

I do not pretend to be a vet, nor do I suggest that these recipes are a cure all for your babies, but if you do everything you can do to keep them healthier, you and your animal child will greet each day with a happy heart. You will have no regrets when, and if they ever have a serious health problem, knowing that you have done everything you can possibly do to make them healthy and content. You will have no regrets when it is time to say goodbye.

You will have fed them foods that God originally intended for them to eat.

If I have helped your animal children live longer, then I have done well by both of you, you and your animal children, and that makes me very happy.

Many people have already started feeding pets table food, or have fed them table scraps all along, which is better than canned food, **if** it is well balanced. But, scraps are not filled with enough nutrition, and we humans do not always get all the nutrition in home cooked meals that we should be getting either, due to the soil conditions of today.

We humans need supplements and so do our pets.

Just spend 20 to 30 minutes, two times a week which is all it takes to help them live longer, healthier lives.

You will have to experiment with how much you feed your child as some kids require more, or less, than another child that is the same size. It depends a lot on the amount of exercise they get.

Always, and I mean always, feed them twice a day, not once a day. YOU don't eat only once a day do you? Of course not.

They are starving in the evening by the time you feed them, and the nutrition is far better for their bodies if distributed twice a day. **Split up their vitamins and minerals and herbs into the two meals also.**

Please experiment with smaller dosages of herbs and vitamins at first, if you want to, and gradually increase it.

My personal selections for additional nutrition

Calcium: use ground egg shells, or Dry Curd Cottage Cheese or Bone Meal.   And I even use Calcium capsules which can be purchased from Health Food stores.

Vitamin C: I buy small packages with 1000 mg. powdered Vitamin C. My favorite has 32 minerals and a B Complex. I give 500 mg. for sure when first changing their nutrition. A little diarhea make take place, but it will not hurt them. They are just not used to it. The body will sluff off what they don't need into the urine.

I give my babies 1000 mg. of vitamin C if they are battling a physical problem or illness. Vitamin C promotes healing.

Vitamin E: 400 I.U. (necessary for healing)

Garlic & parsley gel tabs: Break open one capsule a day. Great for the blood.

Kelp: gel capsules are available

Alfalfa: gel capsules are available

Vitamin A: 10,000 units a day at first, but if carrots are heavily used each day, you can cut down on the vitamin A. There is also Vitamin A in the cod liver oil that I use.

B-12 is necessary for older animals, as they become anemic sometimes due to the lack of vitamins in their food. This especially applies to cats for some reason.

I give my cats and dogs raw beef liver, and raw calves liver, But, always freeze it first (to kill bacteria). If raw turns you off to handle it, microwave it two minutes, after thawing out, then it is easier to cut up into small pieces.

You can give raw chicken, but, freeze it first. I still do not feel comfortable with all the antibiotics fed to chickens. I usually cook all chicken, hamburger & turkey. But if I do give them raw chicken, I make sure it is organically grown, no antibiotics.

Speaking of antibiotics, if you are forced to give a pet an antibiotic, please do them a favor and use **echinacea** herb, and even during the use of this antibiotic always give a little acidophilus to them to restore the proper balance of necessary bacteria in their little stomachs.

Acidophilus should be given once a week anyway for proper balance of bacteria. You know what happens to their stomachs when they eat things that they should NOT be eating, GAS !!

And they throw the proper bacteria balance off in their stomachs when they eat strange things in the yard, yuk.

I have found a wonderful product called **MSM (methylsulfonylmethane),** which is a fundamental source of nutritional sulfur, a naturally occurring

nutrient, which provides flexibility and porosity to cell walls, allowing nutrition "in" and "out". Thereby helping with absorption of vitamins and minerals. I have recently discovered that this sulfur can relieve joint pain.

It has the ingredients that "**used to be**" in our soil, before it became so depleted over the last 50 years. I have seen a noticeable, real improvement in my Cassie's condition after introducing this sulfur to their diet.

It is a proven fact that if vitamins and minerals can and are being absorbed, the body is being fed, and becomes healthier. Tumors in humans and animals have been known to shrink. 1/4 Tsp. per 30 pounds of body weight is all it takes. I know this product is produced in Oregon.

BARLEY GREEN is another wonderful, nutritious health aid, consisting of barley greens, brown rice and kelp. A small amount will be an added benefit 3 times a week.

EMERALD GREENS is so loaded with ingredients you could literally eliminate the health powder. For example: One tablespoon of this powdered super food contains 8,555 mg. per serving of nutrients.

It contains: soy, lecithin, spirulina, apple pectin, apple fiber, barley grass, wheat grass, beet juice powder, bee pollen, ginseng, echinacea, suma powder, ginkgo, grape seed, green tea, and more.

I also give Cassie daily, essential fatty acids, organically grown. **GOLDEN FLAX OIL** - 1,000 MG. and give one capsule (bite it open) daily.

Flaxseed Oil is good, just tastes terrible. Fish Oil tastesbetter.

If you want to pre-prepare a "nutritional powder" to use daily:

Mix: 2 cups nutritional yeast (omit if allergic)
              1 cup lecithin granules (health food stores)
              1/4 cup kelp or alfalfa powder
              1/4 cup bone meal
              1 tsp. of Barley Green
              2000 mg. Vitamin C

To omit the yeast - reduce bone meal to 5 tsp. - add a good multi-vitamin.

Raw veggies: such as chopped parsley, alfalfa sprouts, heat grass, finely grated carrots, zucchini, beets, and apples Cooked only: corn (hard to digest) peas, green beans, broccoli and carrot chunks

Tip: We all know **GARLIC** is great for blood vessels and blood, but did you know garlic cloves, sliced, are great for removing or shrinking warts on dogs.

Place a slice of garlic on-top of the wart and wrap with gauze or ace bandage and pin it on. Leave for two or three days at a time. It really works. Garlic has successfully eliminated the wart completely.

An old Indian remedy is to put a small slice of tomato onto the swollen pore or wart, wrap the same way, and leave it for 12 hours or so and the swelling will go down. It may be possible to reduce the sore area completely if the dog will leave it on longer. They usually won't, as they can feel the drawing power of the tomato, and it may itch.

My mother put two slices of tomato on my cheeks when I had the mumps at 14 years of age. I was in so much pain and so swollen I couldn't get comfortable. She was told by an old Indian woman, to try this, and the next morning, after sleeping all night with tomatoes on my face, the pain and swelling were gone. Like magic. I am now using this remedy on Cassie's enlarged pores which, unfortunately, is a genetic thing. Inbreeding, or vaccines, no doubt. I will probably never know.

For pain relieving measures for arthritis plus good joint care in older dogs, I have found a product in cat and dog health magazines that contains <u>glucosamine HCL and chondroitin sulfate and Vitamin C.</u> The same thing humans are taking for joint pain.

My dachshund has not ruptured a disc, or hurt his back once since I started him on this product called **HCL**. He has a history of herniated discs. Four to be exact.

I am going to introduce you to some recipes that have changed my animal children's lives.

They no longer have gas and bad breath. Other friends that have changed their dogs diets say they no longer crave cat feces, eat rocks or bark dust or eat grass like they used to.

You will see measurable improvements in your children's behavior and .... odors.

The first recipe comes from much research into nutrition, and healing herbs. This recipe I honestly believe, has been the biggest healing force in Cassie's life. I would never dream of eliminating the vitamins and herbs that accompany these healing foods either. Especially the sulfur called MSM.

When you use these recipes in conjunction with herbs and vitamins and the sulfur, you are providing everything that God intended for good health centuries ago, when the land was full of nutritious elements that we need for good health, and when there were no cans of commercial food or bags of kibble. Kibble that loses its flavor and nutrition within hours and days of being opened.

Do not worry about them getting enough hard chewable foods, you can always give them raw or cooked beef marrow bones, which keep them occupied for hours, and they're tasty too. When through with the meat, put a little peanut butter or baby food treats inside the bone, or inside a rubber bone.

CASSIE'S CUISINE

Bake a chicken or turkey. This will make several meals this way. Freeze 1 to 6 cup packages, or more, depending on the size of your animal child's meals. Freeze all the packages that are not being used. Just thaw out a package a day prior to making their weekly meals.
This recipe is for a 15 lb. animal, so adjust accordingly.

Bake about a 14 lb. Turkey or chicken
Strip bones of all the good meat   Use 1 cup per meal
    See chart at back of book
Boil spring water (not tap water)   2 cups
Add the couscous to boiling water   1cup (makes 2 c.)
Turn off heat, let couscous cook itself, just stir
Then:
Juice (juicers make it easier)   4 carrots
1/2   beet (scrub first)
(Or steam the vegetables once in awhile)
1 – 2   (juiced)   apples (no seeds)
1   (juiced)   bunch Parsley
1 or 2   (juiced or grated)   cloves garlic
Add 1 teaspoon expeller pressed oil

Freeze unneeded proportions in baggies for quick defrost
Freeze all but three days meals at a time.

Mix all ingredients together while warm.   My kids love warm food.

Give your pet a squirt of the juicer's juice too, about 4 cc. They learn to like it. I use a vet's plastic medicine syringe. If no garlic cloves are on hand, use garlic powder for flavor. Soy sauce is tasty instead of garlic if you wish.

Continued on next page......

Now add, (always after heating), MSM, vitamins, herbs, Vitamin E, Garlic & Parsley, Vitamin C (essential for healing), HCL (joints), and barley green three (3) times a week.

I add MSM every meal, which helps them assimilate all these nutrients into their organs and skin. Also, to build the immune system. I feel this has been one of the key ingredients to shrinking Cassie's adrenal gland tumors.

If you always include carrots, beets, parsley, and apple you will be giving them the most essential cleansing and nutritious veggies and fruit daily. The beets are a great cleanser.

This ONE diet alone can keep your kids healthy.

The same applies for us humans. So let them eat what Mom and Dad eat please. If it is healthy. Never give them chocolate, it can kill them. Cassie got into some chocolate my son left out and she had to be rushed to the emergency vet and be put into an oxygen chamber. She could not breathe easily or had a tremendous stomach ache, they were not sure. But, I was told at that time that dogs have died after eating chocolate.

Another great time saver and frees you from doing "doggie" dishes every day, is to use paper plates. They cost about $.99 for 100 of them and you use about 60 of them a month for each dog, and believe me, it is so nice not to have to wash their dishes twice a day.

Higgin's Haughty Hash

Here is a recipe, easy to multiply because it uses one unit of each ingredient.

      1 cup turkey, chicken, or lean beef, raw if you wish
      1 cup brown rice (2 cups water)
      1 cup cooked soy beans (canned or pre-cooked)
      1 cup shredded carrots (use juicer if possible)
      1 shredded beet
      1 small bunch shredded parsley or cilantro
      1 small juiced apple (skin okay)
      1 tbl. vegetable oil
      1 tbl. soy sauce

Bring 2 cups of water to boil for every cup of rice, simmer for 45 minute. Add meat, cook a little longer. Add all other ingredients.

Add MSM now.
Biotin (Foster Smith) is a great addition to diet.
1 packet 500 mg. Vitamin C
1 400 i.u. vitamin E capsule

Fazer's Fakitas

1 cup ground chuck (cooked)
1 cup pinto beans or black beans (cooked)
1 1/2 cups cornmeal (6 cups water)
1 tsp. soy sauce
1 clove garlic, crushed
Juice 4 carrots
Juice 1 beet
Juice small bunch parsley
Juice 1 apple
YOU drink the juice
Give pet 1 tbsp. juice w/dropper
1 tbl. vegetable oil
1 tbl. bonemeal
5,000 i.u. Vit A
400 i.u. Vit E

6 cups water to boil - cook cornmeal until fluffy
Add cooked meat and all other ingredients.
Add oil, bonemeal, vitamins, HCL, & herbs at
each meal. Especially the MSM for absorption.
Before food is served add garlic/parsley tab, multi–vitamin,
joint care. Then freeze all but 3 days meals. Do not leave in
fridge more than 4 days. Add vitamins & herbs daily so they
don't lose their value.

16.

Fazer

TOOGOODTOBETRUE TOFU

1	Cup Rolled Oats
4 Oz.	Tofu
2	Raw Eggs
1/4 Cup	Raw Carrots
1 Tbl.	Health Powder or Emerald Green
1 tsp	Olive Oil
1/2 tsp.	Eggshell powder
dash	Salt or soy sauce
small clove	Garlic (crushed)

Boil 2 cups water
Add 1 cup rolled oats, remove from heat
Let it sit, stirring occasionally.
Add Eggs
Add Tofu
Add raw carrots (well shredded or cooked)
Add all other healthy ingredients
Don't forget your MSM, for absorption
Vitamin E
Vitamin C

SASHA'S SIMPLICITY

kitties & canines can benefit from this one

1 Cup	Instant Cream of Wheat
2 Cup	Water
3 Cups	Eggs
1 tsp.	Bone Meal
	or 1/4 tsp. Health Powder
1/4 tsp.	Soy Sauce

You can use oatmeal from your own breakfast or make fresh.

Bring 2 cups spring water to a boil.

Add raw oats, cover pan, turn off heat in 2 minutes.

Let it cook with residual heat for 5 minutes

Stir in raw or cooked eggs, soy sauce & health powder.

This recipe is so handy when nothing is thawed out for your pets in the morning, or you are in a hurry.

MOSES MASH
Another simple breakfast

2 Cups	spring water
1 Cup	Instant Crème of Wheat
1/4 to 1/2 Cup	Chopped Cooked Chicken
1 tsp.	Bone Meal
1/4 tsp.	soy sauce
or	
1 tsp.	soy bean butter

Boil 2 cups water
Add 1 cup Instant Crème of Wheat
Add raw or previously cooked chicken or
Microwave some chicken to put in cereal
Add bone meal
1 tsp. soybean butter

Don't forget their vitamins & herbs for the day.

Solomon's Stew

2 cups	Cooked chicken
5 small	Boiled red potatoes
1 cup	Oat bran
2 cups	Cooked carrots, broccoli, or carrots & green beans Frozen or canned okay
1 cup	Shredded carrots (From juicer preferably) if uncooked
1 Cup	Dry curd cottage cheese (optional)
1 bunch	parsley, shredded
2 small	juiced beets, or cook them
1/2 tsp.	cold pressed safflower, soy or corn oil

Cook vegetables if not juicing, using 3 to 4 cups water.
When veggies are soft,
Add the oat bran, cooked chicken, potatoes and let sit for
5 minutes until soft. Then add remaining ingredients.

Feed twice a day
Add MSM
Vitamin E
Vitamin C
Emerald Greens or Barley Greens

DEWEY'S DELI LOAF

1/4 LB. (1/2 cup)	LEAN BEEF HEART
3/4 CUP	CORNMEAL (Use with lean meat only)
3 CUPS	SPRING WATER
1 CUP	1% OR 2% MILK
2	EGGS
1/4 CUP	CARROTS, PEAS or GREEN BEANS
1	GARLIC CLOVE (crushed)
1/4 tsp.	SOY SAUCE
1 tblsp.	VEGETABLE OIL
1 tsp.	HEALTH POWDER *
400 i.u.	VITAMIN E *

Mix all ingredients together, raw
press into a casserole dish, so it is 1/2" thick
bake at 350 degrees 20 to 30 minutes.

*Add the Vitamin E and health powder preferably after cooking.

21.

MC CLOUDS MEATY MUFFINS

1 lb.	Lean Ground Chicken
4 C	previously boiled red potatoes
1 C	1 or 2% milk
2	Large Eggs
1 Cup	Carrots or Peas, or both
1 clove	Garlic
1 tsp.	Vegetable Oil

Mix ground chicken with potatoes,
add milk and eggs and carrots & peas
Mash all together in a dish.

Take small handfuls and put into a
muffin tin one at a time. Make level
with each muffin holder as there is shrinkage.

Bake at 350 degrees 30 to 45 minutes

These meaty muffins are easy to take
in a refrigerated container, frozen
or ready to use as a meal when traveling

Kentucky Goco

Fast Food at it's Best

1 Cup	Couscous, or Bulgar, or Polenta
1 Cup	1/2 lb. lean Ground Beef
1 Cup	Cooked Carrots or Green Beans
1 tbl.	Soy Sauce, or crushed garlic
1	Juiced or Peeled, pitted, apple

Boil 2 cups water
Add beef, cook for 3 - 5 minutes
Add Couscous, or other grain, stir until mixed
Immediately remove from heat & let sit until thick
Add canned carrots or green beans (cut up)
Add mashed apple
Add soy sauce or crushed garlic

PILGRIM'S TRAVEL PATTIES

2 cup	couscous or oats
4 cups	spring water
1 cup	ground turkey
1 cup	cooked beef liver
1	egg
1 Tbl.	nutritional powder

or take their MSM, & vitamins with you.

1 tsp.	soy sauce
1 clove	crushed garlic
1 Tbl.	soy bean oil or olive oil

Boil water, add cous cous, or oats, simmer 3 minutes
Put into a bowl, add turkey, and beef liver
Add egg
Add soybean oil
Roll into small balls for travel or,
Pat into patties, put one piece of wax paper
in between each, and stack for travel.
Freeze, and carry in an insulated cooler, pack
in ice for longer trips.

I realize that it is difficult to think of cooking food for your animals in a hotel room. But, it will not ruin their health, temporarily, over a one or two week period, to make them eat out of a can or bag.

I have also taken many jars of baby food with me to mix with kibble or canned food, for canine or feline children. Turkey sticks, carrots, spinach, chicken, beef, etc. Plus it is easy, neat to carry and easy to open in the hotel rooms. At least there is a little more nutrition in the baby food than kibble.

Remember, the vitamins, herbs, MSM, and so on are not hard to carry, and they are indispensable in the on going benefits that they provide. Traveling is no excuse to discontinue these nutrients.

If the cooking of fresh food is truly inconvenient, at least give them the nutrients they need, mixed in with the kibble or canned food. Order a dish for them at a fast food restaurant as a last resort. Chicken nuggets always work.

You don't want to set them back so far that it takes weeks to play catch up with their health. I am afraid to let Cassie go without these nutrients for even 2 days, so I really try to plan ahead for her.

TIGGERS TEMPTATION
1981 - 1997

Fresh Beef Liver	1/2 Cup
Fresh Dolphin free Tuna	1/3 Cup
Peas and carrots	1/3 c
2% Milk	1/3 c

Poach the milk (bring to a boil)
Boil water and cook vegetables
for 40 to 45 minutes. Or Steam.

Drop all the tuna, and liver into
the poached milk for a few minutes only.

Take meats out of milk & cool
on a plate.
Flake it all up, mix with veggies

Pour/sprinkle milk over all.

Truffel's Treats

For special treats, with or without a meal.

1 cup whole wheat flour
1 cup corn meal
1/2 cup maple syrup
  or 1/2 cup honey

Mix whole wheat flour, corn meal, and honey together
Mix well by hand
Roll out on a bread board like a big flat cookie
Punch out cookies in whatever shapes you wish
Bake in oven for 10 minutes at 350 degrees

Use these as training treats, or just plain ol' cookie treats.

Great to take on trips for snacks too.

Phoebe's Feast
Feline children will love this one

1 Cup	podarta
2	eggs
2 tbsp	cold pressed safflower oil
1 lb.	ground chicken or turkey
2 tsp.	fresh veggies, including beets
4 tbsp	health powder
2 tbsp.	bone meal

Boil 4 cups water
add podarta
Mix well & simmer for 10 minutes
Add eggs, oil, and remaining ingredients
Your kitty may need Vitamin B-12 (for anemia)
so add raw beef liver, shredded with a knife.
Calves liver can be added also as alternative
Please.... freeze these beef additives first, thaw,
then add. It is excellent for their blood,
especially older kitties.
Even if you add the raw liver to their canned
food you will be doing them a nutritious favor.

Tip: My kitties and doggies also love <u>wheat grass</u> to snack on. You can buy it in health food stores, or in some markets. Grind it up in a juicer also.

If your animal children do not take to the change in diet so abruptly, please, add their canned food (two tablespoons or so) to the food. It will not destroy what you are trying to do at first. They are at least getting all the nutrition in the natural food and vitamins that they need to improve. You can gradually take them off the canned and bagged food. You can also put some water in their dry kibble, let kibble sit for a few minutes to make a gravy, or stick it in the microwave for one minute to soften and get soupy, then add to the new menus.

Most people do not realize that within a few days of opening dry kibble bags, bacteria hits the food, and whatever vitamins ARE in the food evaporate. All while sitting in loosely sealed buckets and sacks. After a few days it is of no value, but they eat it out of hunger, even though it is really not very good, or nutritious. Have you noticed the rotten egg smell of their "gasses' they emit.? There is a reason for that. My dogs never pass gas anymore. Their colon is not full of junk.

Many dogs try to get what their bodies need by eating feces in the yard, sometimes their own. They eat some pretty strange things when their bodies are craving the nutrition it needs, or they are anemic.

Would you eat a week old hamburger, or a month old bowl of rice? Only an innocent, hungry animal child would do such a thing for you. And, besides he will revert back to a natural scavenger nature and just eat it. Animals in the wild eat road kill. So we know their stomachs can handle it. They love raw food.

Back to wondering why your animal children are eating their own feces, other dogs feces, or cat feces in the yard, don't wonder any longer. There is something seriously lacking in their diet. You will see behavior changes when their bodies are getting the nutrition it needs, and is no longer craving vitamins herbs, greens, and nutritional sulfur and herbs.

Personality disorders have been eliminated in human children when their diet is changed. The same thing can happen with your animal children.

They will eat grass, to throw up. Why? Their stomachs are upset, or the bacteria balance is out of whack. When they are given acidophilus you will see a change in that behavior also. BUT, try to give them home grown wheat grass, it is excellent for their health.

Coloidal Silver makes a fantastic antibiotic by the way. I use it to clean Cassie's ears, eyes, tear ducts, and put a drop in her water, which is of course, pure spring water. Keeps her ears clear, and sinuses free of yeast. And doesan excellent job of killing bacteria in the area just below the eyes, where gunk collects. But, do continue to give acidophilus every week when using any antibiotic.

I use an ozone needlepoint ionizer air purifier, which is left on 24 hours a day. Cassie had a serious problem with yeast in her ears, sinuses, and feet (around the nails). I mentioned this previously. I live in an extremely wet Northwest region, lots of mold, mildew, and yeast problems, and it is a constant battle to keep her ears yeast free.

Amazingly, the ozone air purifier has eliminated the yeast problem after 8 years of doctors, allergy specialists, etc. All they could come up with, is what they know through medical training. And, unfortunately most are unaware of natural remedies.

She was even put through an experimental surgery, and nearly died of asphyxiation. A surgery to scrape the cartilage in her nose. She could barely breathe. I have never felt so helpless, and at the same time, guilty, for putting her through that torture. It turned out to be an experimental surgery, which had never been done prior. Who knew? And the next step, as I stated previously, was the cortisone fiasco.

I have struggled for years to keep this precious angel alive and well, but doctors just did not believe in natural medicine until recently, and I don't want anyone else to go through what I have gone through in their search for solutions. There are remedies for their illnesses and sinus problems.

I may not have a Ph.D. after my name, but I have learned from experience, and practice. I have researched natural cures and alternatives for years. I have done all I know to find a cure for my Cassie's condition, or even to prolong her life. That is called practical experience.

I have consulted with many doctors, and the best teaching hospital in the country, but alas, all doctors know is surgery or heavy duty medication, and the side effects can leave them with a poor quality of life, if they survive the anesthesia and terribly invasive surgery.

I turned to alternative medicine, and all doctors are astonished at how well Cassie has done this past year. I needed to learn how to keep my little Cassie girl alive and I just put into practice what I had been using for myself and my children. I believe she is alive today because of her special diet. And all the healing herbs nature has provided us.

My natural pet vets are not surprised, of course, at the turn of events, and believe just as I do, in healing herbs. Some have given me suggestions and help in forming these wonderful healing recipes and the rest comes from studying and reading and using my children to practice on. I have experimented with using the same foods that we humans eat. Well, some of us humans eat.

One thing the natural food veterinarians have taught me is the dangers of vaccinations as pets get older, and I knew vaccinations were dangerous for humans, so why not our pets. A recent TV Program has documented evidence of bad

evidence of bad batches of vaccines, that have caused permanent damage to humans, even death. Ask for the batch number when giving vaccines to any living thing. Consider the age of the animal.

Don't give them rabies vaccines every two years, just because the animal control departments says they have to be vaccinated to be licensed. You can find a natural pet veterinarian that will have your pet excused as they get older, due to their age and condition. He will write a letter for you, to accompany the renewal. I do that every year. They do not need rabies vaccinations more than twice in their entire life.

We don't have measles vaccinations every two years our entire life, or mumps, or polio vaccines every two years. Think about it. It is a way of keeping us coming back over the years to spend money.

I am not suggesting that you never treat your pet with medicine, or let them be vaccinated or operated on, just make yourself aware of alternatives, use your gut instinct after hearing the doctor's prognosis for quality of life, then decide. Do a little research into vaccines.

I prayed all throughout my search for a cure, from doctor to doctor, hospital to hospital, state to state, and I believe I knew in my heart each time I heard their advice, what to do or what not to do.

God cares about these wonderful creatures - He made them.

Please consider taking the time to learn an alternative way of life and alternative foods for your beloved and devoted child. If you want this precious friend and companion to live a longer, healthier life.

She, or he loves YOU more than life itself, and only wants your love in return. What's a little food twice a day for this special kind of love. Where can you find this anywhere else on this planet.

Only God has this kind of unconditional love in His spirit. It is not just a coincidence that His creatures have such loving sweet spirits and have the ability to replace human companionship when we need love. He made them that way. Just for us.

They also have the ability to become our eyes and our ears, or even our legs. He knew we needed them as much as they need us.

He knows how much we humans need love, and can't always find it with other human beings.

I have never really cared for people who do not love animals, there is something missing in their spirit, and it comes through in their lack of compassion for people. No sensitivity to the pain in other people's lives.

We hear every day in the news of the abuse to these wonderful creatures. There is something seriously lacking in people that abuse animals. A heart.

Have fun with your pet, love them and care for them, for we only have a short time with these furry friends. But, you can help them live healthier, during the time we **do** have them.

Don't be afraid to deviate a little from these menus either, to make your life easier, if you run out of certain foods. They like variety and won't notice anything too drastic. Make an oatmeal dinner or breakfast in a pinch.

Just freeze their food in baggies, or bowls. Then you only have to spend 30 minutes once or twice a week actually cooking their meals. You just thaw, and heat the rest of the time.

Make patties, or meatballs for travel, and freeze them ahead of time. If you are afraid you cannot do this while traveling, of course, feed them their canned or bagged food while traveling, but put all of their vitamins and herbs in each meal, because one or two weeks will not hurt their health too much. Unless they have a serious illness, then I would not deviate.

But, return to cleansing their colon as soon as possible. Motor home travel would not present a problem. You can cook their meals easily. The same for some hotels that have kitchenettes.

Baby food in jars, like chicken, turkey sticks, carrots, peas are an easy fix for small dogs.

Now for some tips on airlines.

More and more airlines are refusing to fly animals in their cargo bays these days anyway, so it will become more and more difficult to fly with our pets. But in case you do. Listen up please.

If they are small and fit in one of the newer carrying cases (Sherpa and Samsonite have a nice carrying case), airline approved for under the seat. Then you can reserve a space for them, as the older models do not fit anymore.

Take a small spray bottle with water in it, to spray on their face and in their mouth to refresh them before the airplane takes off and after it lands. Airplanes seem to feel it necessary to turn off the air before and after takeoff and landing. I personally get very stuffy and hot, and if you're hot, they are hot. Especially at floor level.

I give Cassie an ice cube, from my hand, to lick if it gets too warm, that is why I like the mesh carrying cases. They provide more ventilation, they can easily be reached, and they can see their Mama, or Daddy at all times.

I realize this could eliminate all dogs from flying that are over 17 pounds. But if you must fly your child, you really need to see where they have put your precious pet, in the cargo area, before you board. Those luggage handlers are gorillas. Have you seen the damaged suitcases? They don't care whether your precious children are safe or not. I can tell you horror stories about these baggage handlers.

One of the latest disasters, in the Northwest, was a dog who mysteriously disappeared from the plane, from the carrying kennel it was in, and the airport. The kennel was so badly damaged, that it was obvious that something extremely heavy, like A CAR had to have fallen on it, or it dropped from at least 100 feet out the cargo bay doors as the airplane took off or landed. No joke.

These plastic dog carriers are extremely tough and would not have sustained such serious damage, if it had just been bumped or fallen only three feet off the luggage carrier belt.

The pet has never been seen again, to the horror of his loving parents. He was like a child to them. The poor parents are devastated, of course. And never knowing what happened to their animal child is too cruel for words. What an emotionally catastrophic experience. Not knowing what the pet suffered.

Be aware that the air in cargo is not the same as in the cabin at all times, the animals can be placed in dangerous locations in the cargo hold of a plane, and my worst nightmare is, that they are not transferred to the next flight with their parents. Then they sit in a carrier for hours with no water, or ability to potty. Or they can be kidnapped. It is downright cruel.

One Sharpei baby was so traumatized by being left in his carrier for so long his family thought he had gone mad. He tried to bite them when they finally were able to let him out. He was literally sick with fever. And in pain. They had to take him to a vet for help. His bladder could have burst.

The airlines have no excuse for this kind of abuse. One little kitty was lost inside a cargo hold for 30 days, yes 30 long days. Living on condensation dripping inside the aircraft. But no food. How she survived the changes in temperature is amazing.

The airline would not let anyone go in long enough to look for her, so the owners had to get an attorney to file a suit to get them to hold the plane just long enough to search it. Sure enough, their hunch was right, she was still in there. She is alive today, thank God.

The air has been "accidentally" turned off in cargo, therefore, there is no oxygen or cool air getting to them, and they suffocate or die of heat stroke.

One time eight purebred St. Bernards were being flown to a dog show several states away, and the pilot, or copilot turned off the air, (so completely slipped their minds that eight animals were down there), and they all suffocated. A lot of tears, a lot of irreplaceable pets.

Another precious friend, a darling Yorky, was being flown to her destination out of state to be with her mother. Again, the air-conditioning went off, making the air temp climb, in this case to over 125 degrees. We all know the baby would have died, if the pilot had not been a compassionate person. He took a vote, asking all the passengers if they would be willing to land at the closest airport before the animal died of heat stroke.

They all agreed to this, and fortunately the plane landed, an emergency vet was on hand to revive her and give her fluids before she experienced brain damage or death.

Another area of concern I have is not restraining your pets in cars. Or, heaven forbid, not restrained in the back of pickup trucks. Would you let a toddler run around the back of a truck, unrestrained, in cold, wet, or hot temperatures. I seriously doubt it. They lean so far over the side of the truck sometimes you know they are going to be thrown out in an accident or thrown out just turning too suddenly. Some states now have laws against this, finally. One day I parked in a mall parking lot, and what do I see, a black dog, tied in the back of a truck, in the sun, with nothing to stand on but the hot metal bed of the truck. She was trying desperately to get her feet off the bed, but could not do it. I threw some cold water on the bed until her unthinking owner came out and drove off with her, still standing on the hot bed.

As for inside the car, or truck, please buy an inexpensive seat harness for your precious pet, and as for the smaller pets, put them in a secure car seat beside you. I use a really cute car seat with a sheepskin lining. Or use a plastic crate type which is inexpensive. Put a pillow and quilt, or sheepskin in it for comfort.

I also hang my airline sherpa bag from the head rest (for small pets) so they can sit up high while safely restrained, and they can look at all the cars and people.

Cassie and Higgins love to people watch. If people stare at her long enough she sits up and waves. I love it. Of course, people love it too. They usually wave back.

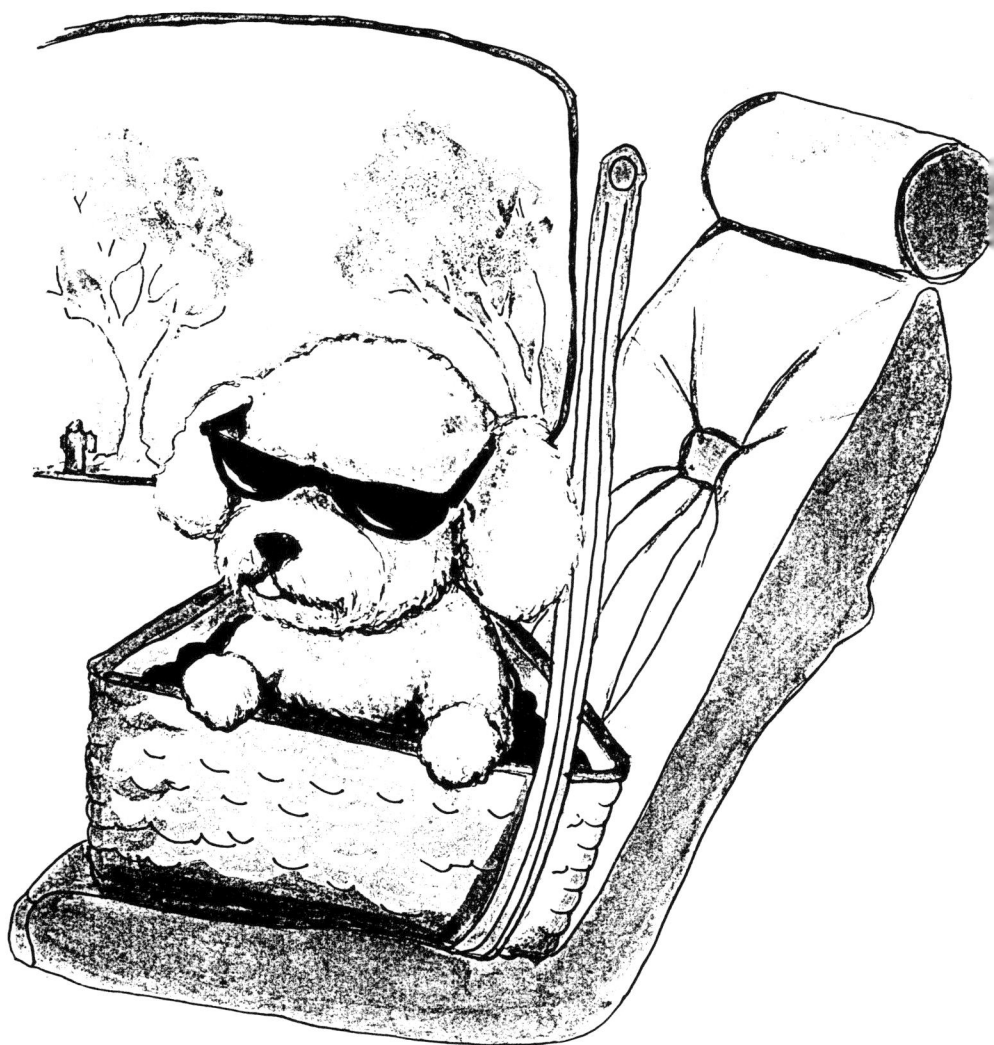

When we go through McDonalds, Burger King or Taco Bell for instance, she honestly believes that we are given food because she waves excitedly at the order taker in the window. They, of course, give her snacks for this cuteness. She has made many friends at fast food drive throughs with her sweet friendly spirit. She is worth a few McNuggets of course.

The following is another remedy for your tiny pets, older pets, arthritic pets, or just plain spoiled animal children.

They love to go walking with you, but if you have hesitated because of your baby's bad hips or arthritis, and they cannot walk as far as you can, I have a solution. I have purchased a baby stroller (2nd hand for a few dollars if you do not have the money), a stroller large enough to hold 2 little dogs, and when they get tired of walking, I just put them in the stroller to rest for a few minutes. Or one rides, and one walks, while I continue on my merry way, getting the exercise I need, at the speed that I need to go, and they absolutely love to feel the wind on their face, while enjoying the sunshine. And of course, just being with you is what it is all about to them. Don't worry about lookin' dorky, who cares.

You are their whole world remember, so whatever you do to include them in your activities, makes them that much happier. I absolutely adore taking walks with them. They are really good company and they don't ever argue about which direction we should go.

I take along a bottle of water for them and myself, a spray bottle for their face, a sun visor that is especially made for their size, to shade their eyes in hotter weather (you can purchase these in pet shops). You can now walk for miles with your animal children. The stroller comes in handy when the asphalt gets too hot also. But, I have to admit I usually do not take them out when it is that hot. Many people do not realize that their little foot pads are not made of teflon.

Their little legs in some cases just can't walk as far as we can. It also helps them work up to longer walks with you over a period of weeks if they're out of shape. I just wish Oregon had sunshine more than two months out of the year, I could enjoy this activity more often. Having to clean up two little dogs that have tromped through mud and wet grass is not exactly fun every day.

I have been stopped over and over by people in cars saying "What a great idea. I have an older dog that cannot walk as far as I can and I have not been able to take her with me." well, now you can.

As you can see, I try to fit them into my lifestyle, using whatever means possible, and make having animal children a happy experience. They can be such a joy. Just don't expect too much from them the first six months. Those can be trying times, but if you learn that they truly have feelings, and they are sensitive to your emotions the bond will become stronger.

Cassie &
Higgins ready
To Roll

I love my pets so very much that I just wanted to share with other animal lovers, whatever knowledge that I have accumulated over the years.

Don't ever let others intimidate you into not doing something creative, or fun with your babies. I don't let anyone influence me that way. I feel that these little ones are the most important people in my life, or my family's life, so I do not care what other people think. My animals think they are people anyway.

I personally get a huge kick out of seeing a big German Shephard wearing a sun visor, sitting up straight as an arrow in the front seat of a jeep feeling so human it is incredible. They really feel important. It is too cute for words.

Most people really want a healthy and safe life for their animal babies. So, If I can help ONE of your animal children live a longer, healthier and safer life, I am a happy Mom.

I hope I have taken you forward to a better life for your pets, a little bit at a time anyway. Using some creative ideas to make life a little more fun.

Once you have learned to fix their meals in 20 minutes two times a week, or 35 minutes once a week, thawing out what you need when you need it, it really **becomes a part of your routine, and when you see the miraculous change in your pet's health and skin, you** will never want to return to the fast food, easy fix, bagged or canned food routine.

LAST, BUT NOT LEAST, FLEAS !!!

I cannot finish this book without giving you one of the most important findings of all.

Did you know people are paying hundreds of dollars every year to rid their pets, homes, and yards of the dreaded FLEA. Of course you knew that. No one wants fleas in their houseor on their pets.

I have a wonderful tip for you, and it is as non-toxic as I can find. Remember good old borax. Our mother's and grand-mothers used in all our wash cycles. Probably for a hundred years, who knows. Well, now you can clean fleas right out of your home, be rid of fleas FOREVER!

All you do is buy a big box of Borax. Pour a flour sifter full of borax, then walk around your whole house sifting lightly onto the carpet, and under furniture and seat cushions.

Then walk out into the yard, and sift it about 20 feet out all around the perimeter of your house, into the grass and flowers, as it will not kill plants. Fleas will be dehydrated and die in a few days. Don't worry about what you look like, your neighbors already think you've lost it, with the stroller idea. I gave up a long time ago caring about what other people think. I have to do what is best for my animals, so I just do what I have to do to make it better. This is the most wonderful discovery that I have made in years, as fleas are a plague to the animal world. Pest companies will charge you big bucks to do the same thing I just taught you to do. They also use a borax based product, but won't tell you about it.

After sifting borax around, rake it (rug rake)or sweep it into the base of the carpet and leave it alone for 24 hours. Then vacuum the surface of the carpet (set level on High) and vacuum all the furniture that you sprinkled, and all the fleas that were in the house will die of dehydration very quickly. But, do this one more time three weeks later, just the carpet and the yard, to kill any fleas that hatched later, and you will never have fleas again. It is absolutely heaven to know that no more flea infestations will occur in my house or on my animals. It has been three years since I first tried this. I have not had any fleas survive, if they have been brought in.

If you are afraid of the borax, that it may dehydrate your animal, or dry their skin, don't let them lay directly on the borax until you rake it into the base of the carpet.

A Naturopathic remedy: Mix 4 cups water, 4 tbl. Rosemary, 4 tbl. Eucalyptus, 4 tbl. Fennel, 4 tbl. Yellowdock in a pan, simmer into a tea, cool, pour into a spray bottle as needed and spray on your pet. Discontinue if it irritates their skin.

The flea treatments that veterinarians are recommending these days are deadly poisonous.

Read the labels of the flea spots for cats and dogs. Read the labels of the cans of flea sprays. They say "If you get the liquid on YOUR hands or skin, wash immediately" It is poison.

Or the label states "Don't breathe the fumes from the spray bottles". "Flush eyes immediately if you accidentally spray the poison into them". Does this make any sense to you.

Do you get the picture? Are our pets any less vulnerable to these poisons than we are? What makes their skin and eyes more able to tolerate the poison and fumes than we are. They are NOT ABLE to tolerate it. We are poisoning our pets every year, as their skin is even more sensitive than ours. They don't have the layers of skin we have for protection. They have fur for protection from the elements.

These poisons are penetrating their skin, being absorbed into their livers, kidneys, adrenal glands, bladders, lymph glands, etc. It may even be causing heart disease.

Then we wonder why our precious pets are developing heart problems, tumors, and the same diseases we humans get. We would not stand directly under a pesticide spray. Why should they be subjected to this insanity.

But, it makes money for the veterinarians, to be able to sell these products. 80% of all the flea killers are dispensed by vets. A few years ago only about 10% of flea products were sold by vets. It is a big money maker.

Please do not put these poisons on your cats and dogs, there is an alternative. Everything takes a little time when first preparing natural alternatives, but it will be worth it I promise you. We will see our animal babies living 25 years or more one day. Thousands of years ago, people lived to be 900 years old. They had no polution in their environment. So we have to at least try to stop the polution in our homes since we have no control over the rest of the world.

Once you realize that there **are** alternatives in life, and we do not have to be a captive audience for doctors and veterinarians to practice on, you will feel a freedom that you have never felt before. You cannot put a price on good health. It feels so good to spend the money on their food, rather than on doctor bills. It is called Preventative Medicine.

Spend more time and energy on your pet's eating regimen, health aides and supplements, and you will save hundreds and even thousands of dollars every year on vet bills. Heaven forbid your animal baby ever develops a serious, life threatening disease or illness. You too may have to make a life or death decision when a doctor gives you his prognosis. When you are faced with the possibly of losing your best friend, you go into a survival mode. Instinctively I knew there had to be an alternative. She deserved all I had to offer. And you are reading the outcome of my years of study. Cassie is still with me due to natural sources.

No matter whether you start now, or start a month from now, it will benefit your precious friend at any stage of their life.

Starting a puppy out on natural foods would be the best of course, but you CAN teach an older pet to love this food. Mine love it, so will yours.

Above all, you will extend the life of the best friend you have ever had. You have made a 15 to 20 year commitment to this wonderful, trusting, loyal companion, so shouldn't that commitment include caring for them to the best of our ability.

THANKS MOM
FOR LOVING ME,

Cassie

Suggested Food Measurements

5 – 15 lbs.	1/2 c. – 1 c.
20 – 25 lbs.	About 3 c.
30 – 40 lbs.	About 4 – 5 c.
50 – 60 lbs.	About 5 – 7 c.
80 – 100 lbs	Whatever he wants ! At least 9 – 10 c.

If your child starts to gain weight adjust the portion down or add more protein (meat), or lentil or black beans, cooked, to their meals.

If your kids seem hungry at night, give them a snack of tofu cheese or scrambled eggs, or low fat cottage cheese, any protein type food, that fills anybody up.

Reference Page

Calcium	Page 8
Vitamin C	Page 8
Vitamin E	Page 8.
Garlic & Parsley	Page 8
Kelp	Page 8
Alfalfa	Page 8
Vitamin E	Page 8
B-12	Page 9
Beef Liver	Page 9
Echinacea	Page 9
Acidophilus	Page 9
MSM	Page 9
Barley Green	Page 10
Emeral Greens	Page 10
Flax Oil	Page 11
Nutritional Powder	Page 11
Raw Veggies	Page 11
Garlic	Page 11
HCL	Page 12
Vegetables for Juicing	Page 14
Wheat Grass	Page 29
Coloidal Silver	Page 30
Ozone Air Purifier	Page 31
Vaccines	Page 33
Freezing the Food	Page 35
Airline travel	Page 36
Car Seats & Safety	Page 39
Using a Stroller	Page 40
Fleas	Page 43

It is not my intention to promote or endorse any of the products mentioned in my book, nor do I make any claims of cures for diseases.

Everything I have suggested in this book, I have personally used.

This is a book of resources, and suggestions for good nutrition only. Please take your animal child to a naturopath for any physical condition that is questionable. Then get your baby on the path to a natural, healthy life.

If just one thing in this book has made a big difference in your little one's life, or helped you become a better parent, please pass it on to someone else. We must get the word out to our friends. Alternative medicine is the only way to stay out of hospitals.

Please copy, then complete this order form to purchase another book, or send inquiries about where to find certain supplements, herbs, msm and the ozone air purifiers that I use.

Name_____

Address_____

City, State_____

Zip Code_____

Item of Interest_____

Send to:
Kaye-Hughes Publishing
7119 SW Locust Street
First Floor
Portland, Oregon 97223
(503) 977-9319

E-mail address: **broker26@juno.com**
Website: **www.dogpages.net/dognatural/index.html**